"We are Leeds"

The Leeds United photo book – from the 1960s to the present day

An official Leeds United Football Club Publication

First Published in Great Britain by GreenPark Publishing, 151 Wick Road, Brislington, Bristol, BS4 4HH

ISBN 0-9537444-5-0

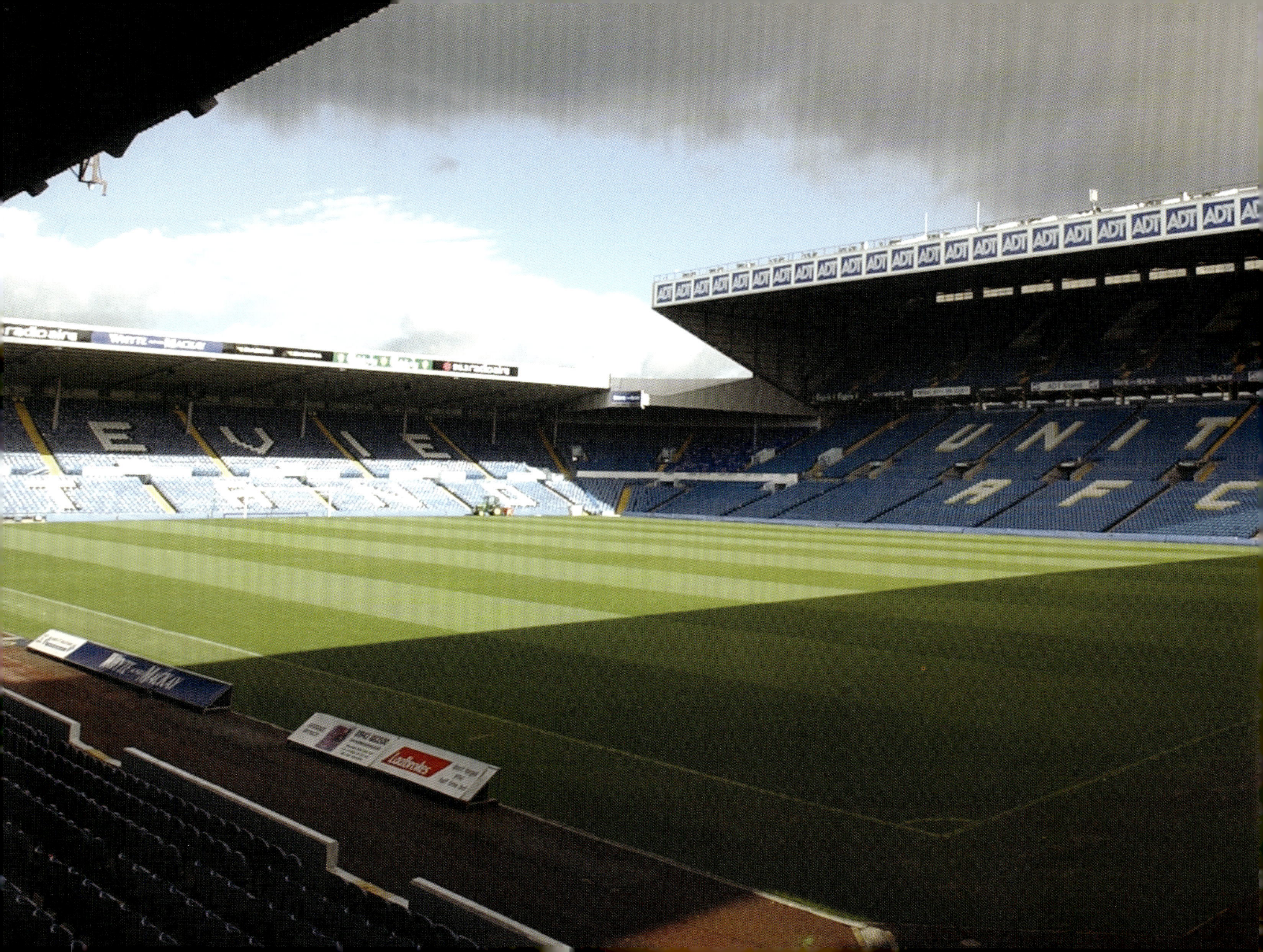
ADT
radioaire
UNIT
AFC
Ladbrokes

Excited and anxious I await my dream
To escape, applaud and embrace my team
Opening day I can always trust
It's just for this high that I crazily lust
Return of our hero does brighten the days
Just briefly my troubles get lost in the haze
The grace from the field arouses the crowd
Reflects on the days when I was quite proud...

Words spoken by Robert De Niro as Gil Renard.
Opening dialogue from The Fan, directed by Tony Scott,
based on the book by Peter Abrahams, screenplay by
Phoef Sutton © 1996 Manadaly Entertainment.

Introduction

Someone once said that being a supporter of a football club is rather like being in a marriage, except that you have less control over how things work out and divorce is much harder and more traumatic.

Certainly Leeds United fans have become very used to the football equivalent of 'for richer, for poorer, in sickness and in health', especially over the last few years when there has been an overdose of 'poorer' and 'sickness'.

So it seems like a good time to remind ourselves of why, against all logic, we continue to support our club, no matter what happens. We don't always enjoy it. We get very angry and frustrated at times. We even threaten to walk away. But something intangible keeps us coming back.

It's partly the magic of football, but more particularly it is the identification with one club, its players and managers, its ground and its history. Above all, it's the feelings shared with the other people who travel long distances, sacrifice time and pay their cash each week for 90 minutes that can fill you with joy or leave you in abject misery, swearing never again...until next time.

The Varley family, John and son Andrew, have been photographing Leeds United since the early days of Don Revie, and here we try and capture something of the essence of the club through their pictures.

It is not a conventional history, nor even a book of the most important players or moments. Many of the big names are here, but so are some of the lesser lights who have passed through Elland Road without leaving much of an imprint. Some of the most memorable moments of the last 40 years are captured for all time, but also some of the trivial, often humorous events that you forget until reminded.

Some of the contents have been selected just because they are great photographs, some because they show scenes fans don't normally get to see, and some because they capture an instance that is powerful in itself but would normally only rate as a footnote in a Leeds United book.

Mostly they have been chosen because they reveal something of the people – managers, players and fans – who have helped and continue to help make Leeds United a very special club.

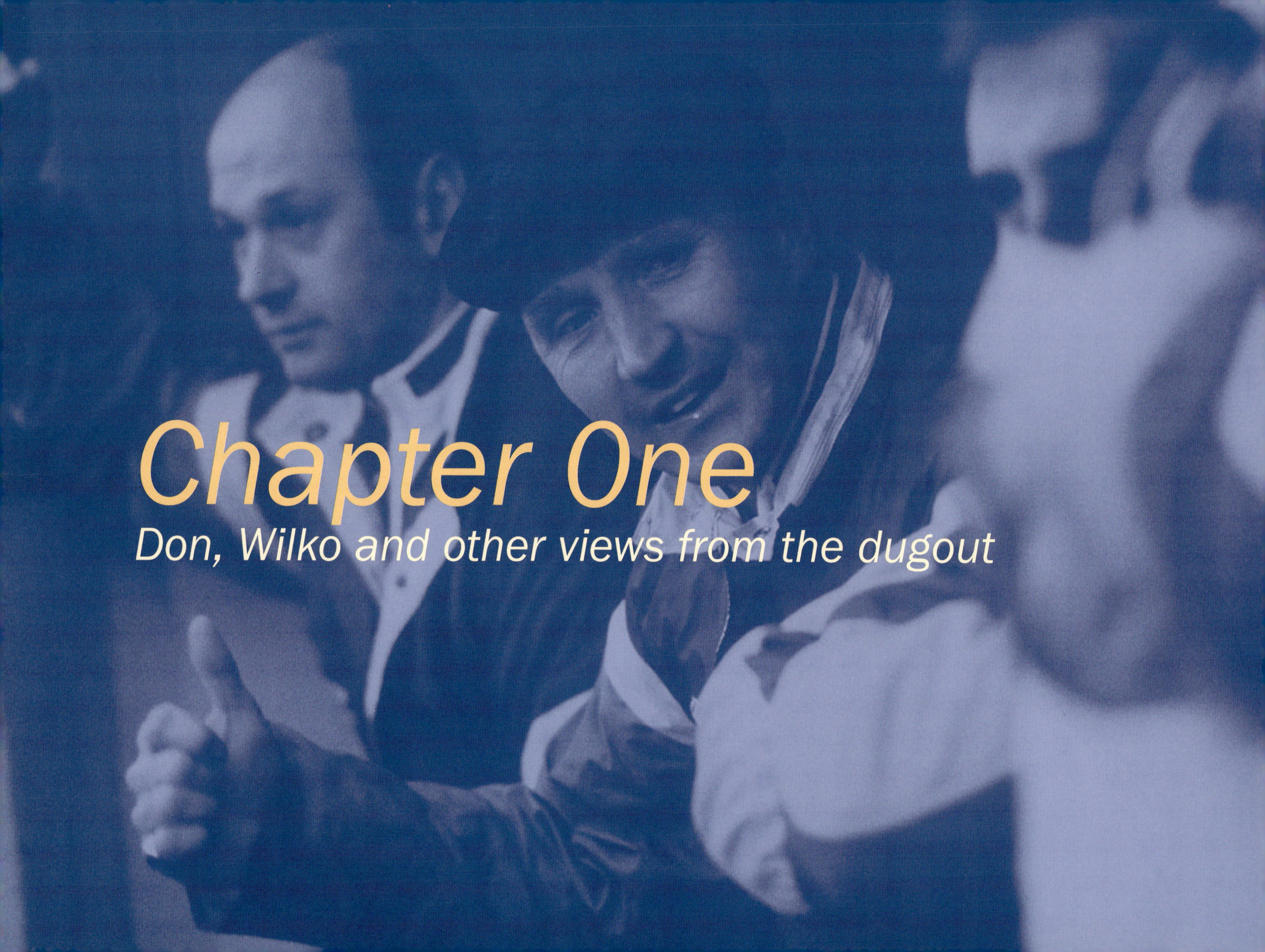

Chapter One

Don, Wilko and other views from the dugout

Mention Leeds United and it won't be long before the name Don Revie comes into the conversation.

It was Revie who took an ailing, under-achieving lower division club and turned it into a force to be reckoned with, in Europe as well as England. Symbolically changing the strip to mimic the great Real Madrid, Revie let it be known early that he would never be content with mid table. In ten years he won the league championship twice, the FA Cup, the League Cup and two European Fairs Cups (now the UEFA Cup). He built a team of great players, arguably one of the best club sides in Europe.

Without Don Revie there would not be a Leeds United as we know it and ever since, managers and players have been trying to live up to the 'Revie era'.

Howard Wilkinson was so convinced that burden was holding the club back, he took down all the memorabilia around Elland Road. He took over a club that was again languishing out of the top flight, worked to a master plan that was at times ruthless and became only the second manager to take Leeds to the league title.

Other managers have tried to emulate those achievements but with the exception of David O'Leary in what is now considered a bitter-sweet period, none has come close.

So, as we tip our hat to the people who have filled one of the hottest and most demanding seats in football, we start inevitably with the man who first put Leeds United on the map.

A master tactician as a player, Don Revie revelled in management where he could put all his ideas into practice. His preparations were thorough to the point of obsession, and his will to win at times meant the beautiful game had to give way to pragmatism.

Yet the ultra professional was also ironically one of the most superstitious men ever to sit in a dug-out. His 'lucky' blue suit wore thin and on the bus going to matches he always kept an eye out for a bride, believing a sighting would bring good fortune. Leeds had been bridesmaids too often!

To Revie, Leeds United became not so much a club as a family. He showed as much interest in a newly signed junior as to the stars and his paternal devotion to all his players was rewarded with a loyalty that survives to this day.

Revie surrounded himself with an outstanding staff and when it came to crunch moments, like extra-time in the FA Cup final, each knew exactly what his job was. But, as always, at the hub of it all was the manager.

Renowned trainer Les Cocker was an invaluable aid to Revie and left Leeds four weeks after the manager to join him on the England staff.

Don Revie took his football seriously but always welcomed the chance to toast success. By the start of the following season, however, it was starting from scratch as though they had achieved nothing.

Leeds' adoring fans knew Revie was the mastermind behind their many triumphs in the sixties and seventies but he always made sure the players and backroom staff got their share of the glory. Here he addresses the fans outside Leeds Town Hall.

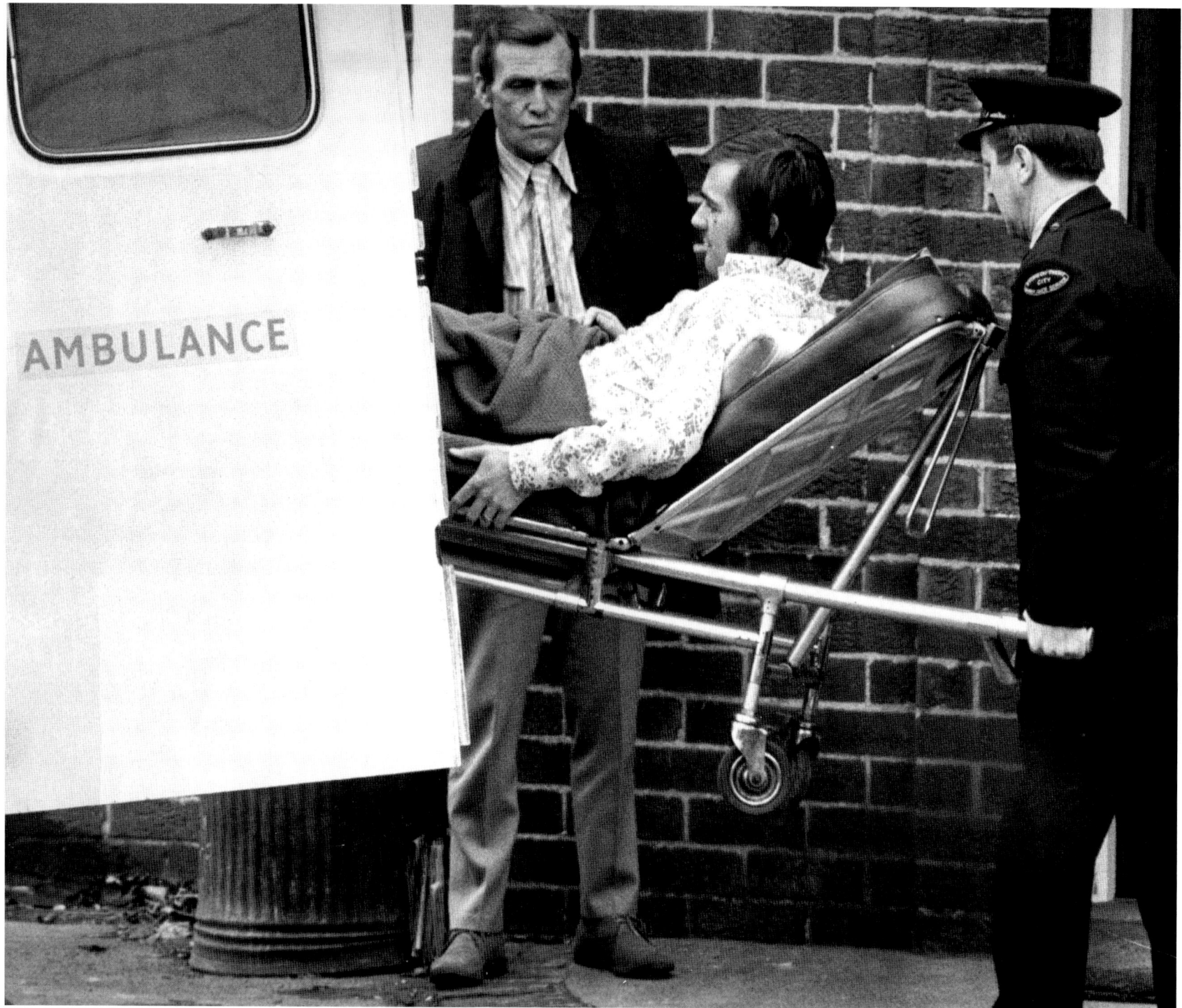

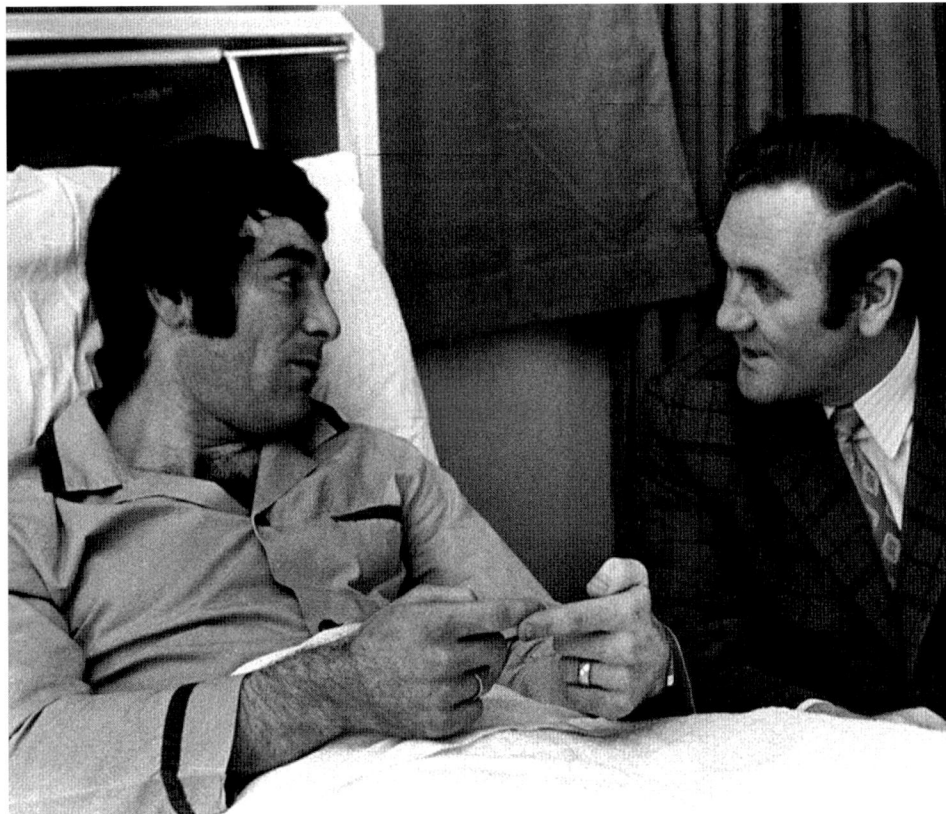

As a Leicester player Don Revie missed the 1949 FA Cup final through injury so when Terry Cooper broke his leg against Stoke to lose out on Leeds' 1972 Wembley triumph, he made sure the England full back was included in the celebrations. Revie also made time for Nigel Davey, the reserve full back who should have taken Cooper's place but broke his leg in a reserve game the same day.

Revie always made time for adoring fans...

...but his natural home was in the dressing room with his 'family'.

Nothing distracted Revie's concentration, neither
the weather...

...nor the visit by star comedian Eric Morecambe,
a director of Luton Town, who appears to be
using the 'Manager of the Month' presentation to
try to lure the Leeds boss to Kenilworth Road.

Any manager was going to find it hard to take over Don Revie's side. Brian Clough, a fierce critic of Leeds United's tactics and style, would find it impossible. He should never have been appointed and after 44 days the players made sure he was sacked. The abrasive Clough always claimed the pay-off set him up for life.

Smiles were few and far between during Brian Clough's reign at Elland Road. Even at the Charity Shield he is a figure on the edge of the group. But if you tell some of the best players in Europe to throw away their medals because they don't deserve them, you will find it hard to win friends and influence people.

'Gentleman' Jimmy Armfield was the man who picked up the post-Clough pieces and led the side to the European Cup final. After 568 league games for his home-town club, Blackpool, Armfield is a football man through and through, and he started to rebuild an ageing side, bringing in players like Tony Currie, Brian Flynn, Ray Hankin and Arthur Graham, but an impatient board made another change before he had chance to finish the job.

Ex Celtic boss Jock Stein lasted one more day than Clough before he left to manage Scotland.

Jimmy Adamson may have made Tommy Docherty laugh, but after one reasonably successful season, Leeds United started to go into decline.

Leeds turned to players who had been successful under Revie – Allan Clarke, Eddie Gray and Billy Bremner – hoping some of the magic had rubbed off.

The fans were overjoyed as Clarke took the applause after Leeds beat Brighton, thinking the points would keep them up, but defeat at West Brom and victory for Stoke meant relegation for the first time in 18 years.

In 1987 Billy Bremner came within 20 minutes of taking Leeds to the FA Cup final and ten minutes of promotion via the play-offs but a year later, with the team struggling, he too was sacked.

Eddie Gray twice had to pick up the baton as Leeds manager in difficult circumstances. In the eighties he was developing a young side full of talented individuals but the board ran out of patience.

In the aftermath of the club's financial meltdown under Peter Ridsdale, Gray had again to jump into the breach following the sacking of Peter Reid, but the team ran out of time.

With Leeds in danger of free-fall, the board looked round for a saviour. Used to applicants who were desperate to get the job, the directors were somewhat taken aback by Howard Wilkinson, who interviewed them and told them how it had to be if he was to move from Sheffield Wednesday. But they were impressed and Sergeant Wilko's era had begun.

An intellectual, with a reputation as somewhat dour, Howard Wilkinson was in fact a witty man, who paid the same attention to detail as Don Revie. His lack of 'sound-bite' philosophy robbed him of some popularity but he built a team that was greater than the sum of its parts and walked off with the championship trophy.

Wilkinson struggled to build on his title success, perhaps concentrating too much on the youth and junior structure. George Graham came and went as the club became a Plc.

Having been with Graham as a player at Arsenal and assistant manager at Elland Road, David O'Leary was eager for his first chance in charge. He rode a wave of optimism and euphoria to European semi-finals but behind the scenes the dream was turning into a nightmare and four managers in two years have had to try to dig a hole in the sand with the tide coming in.

There are times when the tension gets to everyone…

...but it's easy to smile when you are beating Manchester United.

There are moments when you know it is not
going to be your day.

As United start again from scratch, the burden
of turning round one of the biggest clubs in the
country falls to Kevin Blackwell.

Chapter Two

In the heat of battle

We all enjoy the great moments in football – the goals, the incredible saves, the brilliant flashes of skill.

But equally dramatic are those incidents that over the years have provided photographers with some of their best images – spectacular tackles, painful injuries and those confrontations with referees that can be heated or humorous.

Over the years John and Andrew Varley have captured some incredible images from the very heart of the Leeds action.

Back in the sixties and seventies, when you had to go to the swimming pool to see diving, tackles tended to be a bit fiercer and players learned to give it out as well as take it...

...although sometimes they just had to take it.

Referees were far less 'card happy' and the secret was to walk away innocently.

Some fouls are seen by everyone except the referee. In this classic sequence from the 1975 European Cup final, Bayern Munich skipper Franz Beckenbauer scythes down Allan Clarke in the area. The only person who didn't think it was a penalty was French referee Michel Kitabdjan. It was one of many mistakes that cost United the trophy they most coveted and, on the night, deserved.

Referees may have clamped down in recent years but some tackles look painfully similar to those of an earlier era.

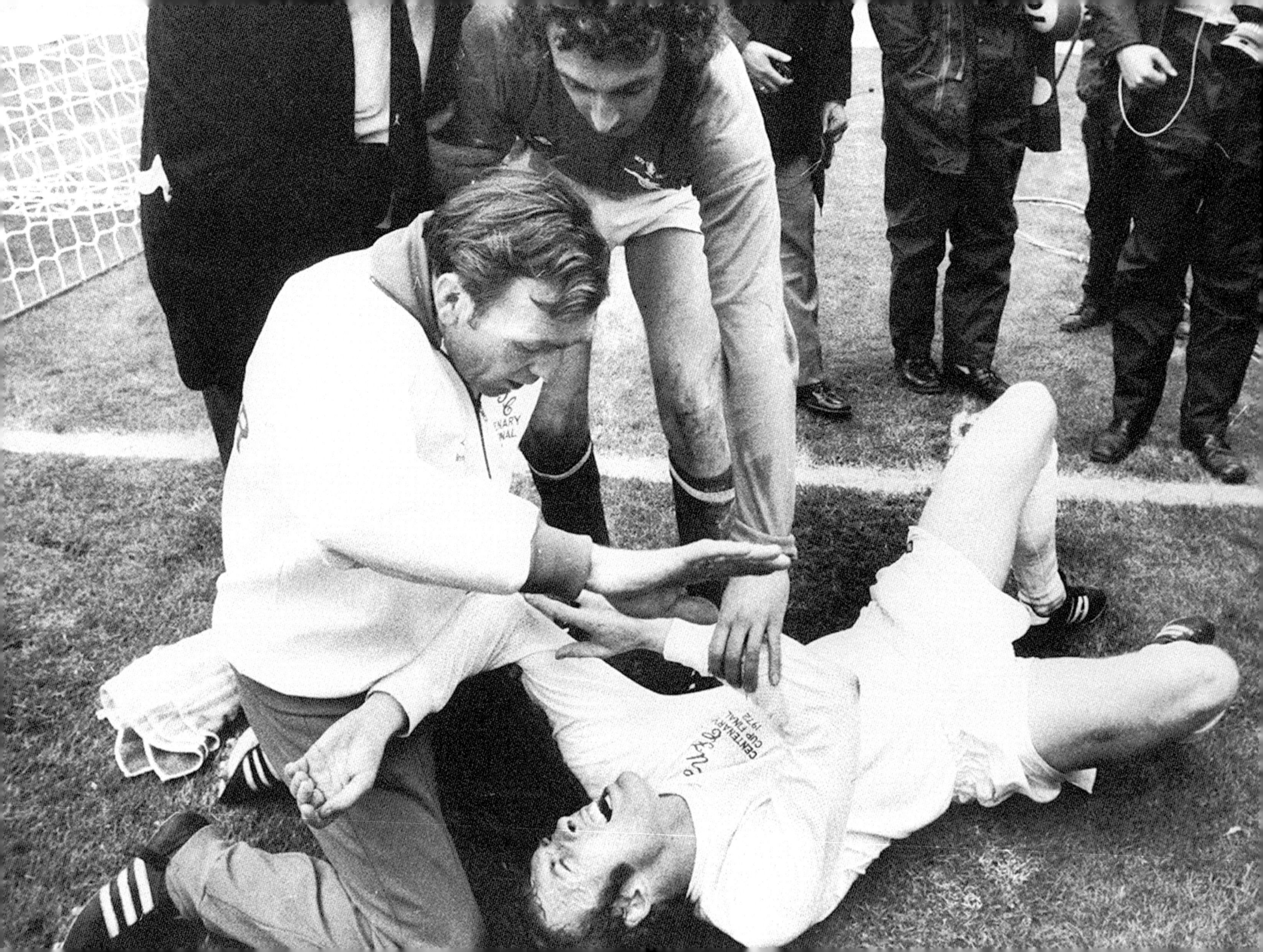

Mick Jones's dislocated elbow in the 1972 FA Cup Final is perhaps Leeds' most famous injury. It happened with just two minutes to go and he was still receiving treatment when the team went up for the Cup, but Norman Hunter helped him up Wembley's 39 steps to receive his winners' medal from the Queen.

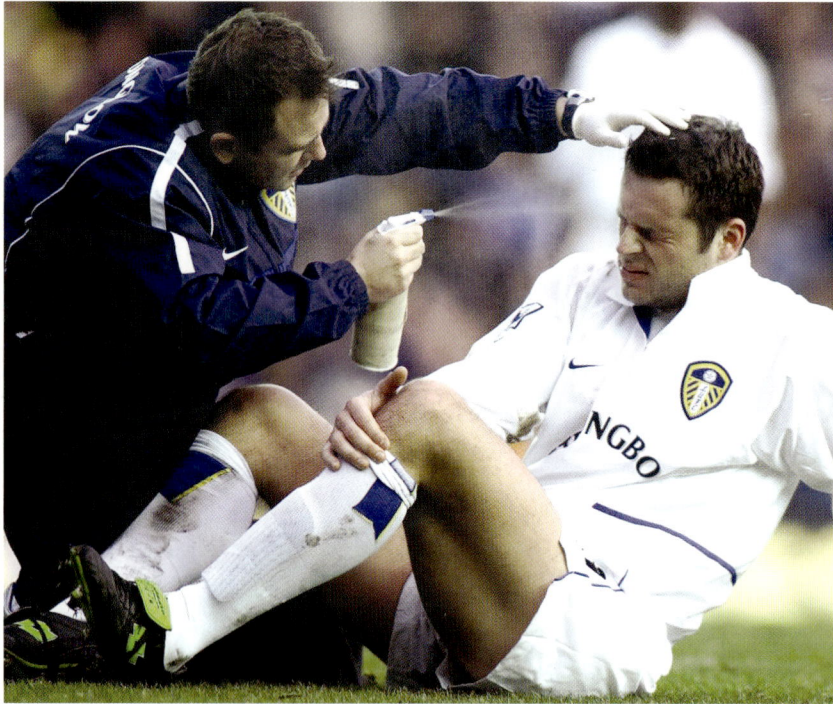

It used to be the freezing 'magic sponge' on the back of the neck, now it's the spray in the face that brings an instant cure.

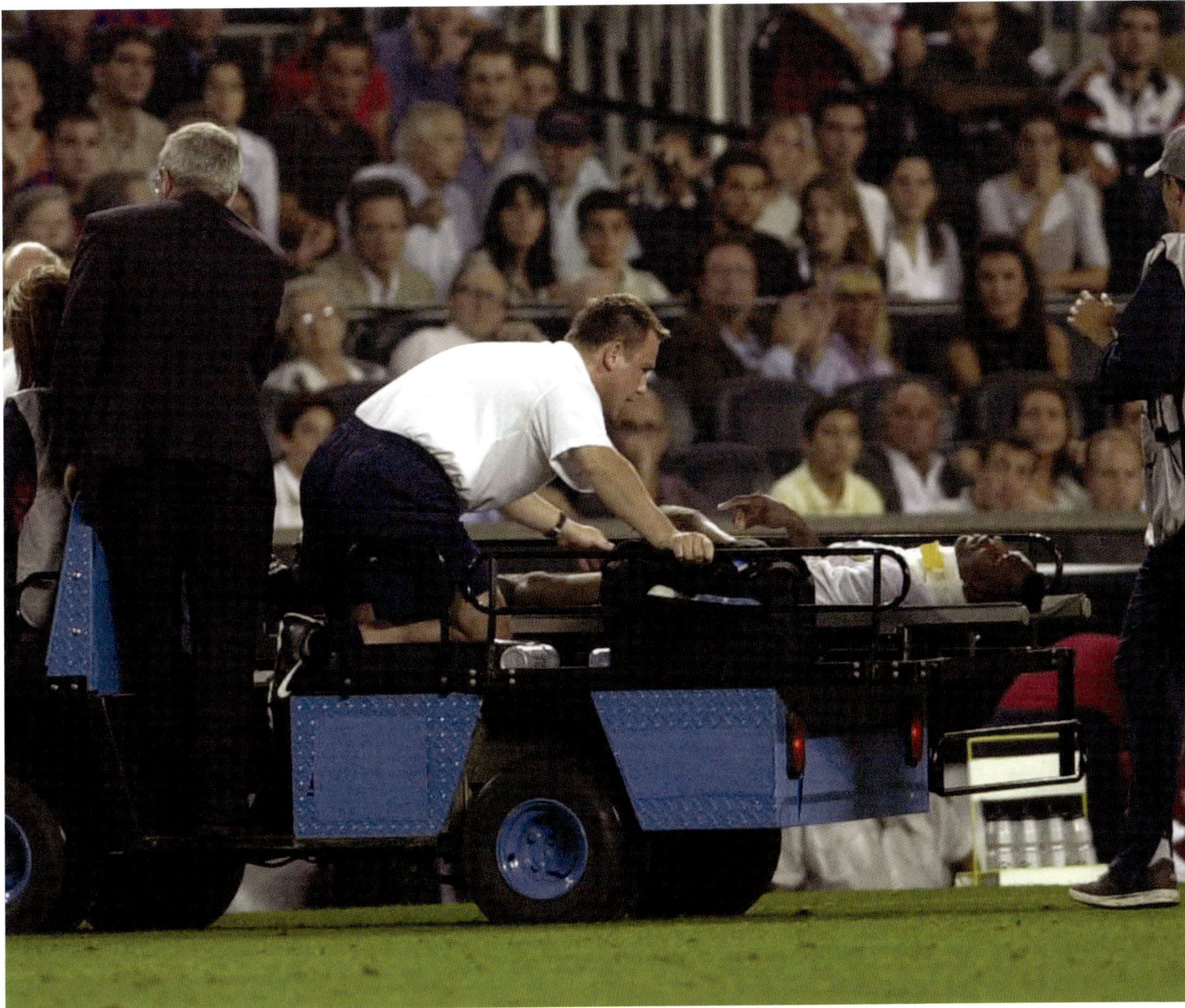

But sometimes it is not enough. Leeds fans were left anxious as Lucas Radebe was stretchered off with his neck in a brace during United's Champions League match in Barcelona. Fortunately fears that the South African was seriously injured were quickly allayed and he returned to playing two games later.

Ouch!

David Batty was known for his uncompromising tackles that opponents certainly felt, but sometimes he had to take it too.

'Batts' limps off against Newcastle. It proved to be his final game for Leeds.

Once the refs did the finger wagging and the players like Norman Hunter looked innocent...

...now it's often the other way round.

Billy Bremner was often gobsmacked at the decisions...

...he wasn't alone, although Alan Smith seems resigned to his fate.

Norman Hunter had a special relationship with referees and players. He had a reputation as one of football's 'hard men' but the fact that he was always quick to apologise meant most of them liked him and gave him the benefit of the doubt.

It's hard to convince any fan that the ref is on
their side and even when he is trying to sort out
a mass brawl, be gets little sympathy.

But when he comes out wearing your team's shirt…!

Chapter Three

Superstars to journeymen – it's all about the players

While managers can stamp their style on a club and directors have the power to make or break, when it comes right down to it, the fans are most interested in the players, the people whose skill, passion, determination or mistakes can make the difference between glory and disappointment.

Some become legends, others are the vital cogs without whom the stars could not operate, a few fail to live up to expectations.

The big names live on in the memory long after they have stopped playing, others are forgotten almost as soon as they leave the club, but they too have played a part in the history of Leeds United.

Think Leeds, think Billy Bremner. The diminutive Scot epitomised everything about Don Revie's Leeds United. Skilful, combative, he had a heart as big as Elland Road and a will to win that was insatiable. As skipper, the red-haired dynamo was Revie's alter ego on the pitch. Nothing distracted him from the job in hand, not even a giant Womble. No wonder they built a statue to him.

Fans remember the Bremner tackles and
tantrums but the real secret of his success was
his footballing talent. He was a midfield genius.

And even those too young to have seen him play
were moved when he died two days short of his
55th birthday.

Don Revie's side could score goals of every type – Peter Lorimer's 90 mph thunderbolts...Johnny Giles's perfectly placed passes into the net...

...Allan 'Sniffer' Clarke nipped in to tuck them away from close range...

...and Mick Jones, Clarke's perfect foil, hammered them home from all over.

But the side had great defenders as well, like Paul Madeley, the Rolls Royce of players.

Big Jack Charlton was the rock at the heart of United's defence...

...but he could be as dangerous in the opponents' box as he was solid in his own.

No one has given greater service to Leeds United than Eddie Gray, as player, coach and manager. One of the 'nice guys' of football, Gray was also one of the most talented players of his generation, with dribbling skills matched only by George Best. Don Revie memorably commented: "If Eddie Gray ran on snow, he wouldn't leave a footprint."

Part of Don Revie's brilliance was his ability to keep strengthening with players like Joe Jordan, Trevor Cherry and Gordon McQueen.

Even when Leeds were fighting to get back into the top flight, there were players who could get the fans off their seats.

Terry Connor

Tony Currie

Tommy Wright

Arthur Graham...

...and the greatest favourite of them all, John Sheridan.

When Don Revie started to rebuild Leeds, he brought in Bobby Collins, a tiny, competitive, immensely talented midfielder. In his turn Howard Wilkinson persuaded Gordon Strachan to bring his fiery genius to Elland Road and another new era was under way.

Wilkinson created one of Leeds' best midfields when he combined the guile and enthusiasm of Gordon Strachan with the youthful promise of David Batty and Gary Speed, and the silky passing of Gary McAllister. They were the heartbeat of the 1992 Championship-winning side.

Carl Shutt and Lee Chapman might never make it into a top ten list of world strikers but they scored many important goals in the Championship season. But none was more vital than John Newsome's stooping header at Sheffield United, the day the title was clinched.

95

David Batty became a Leeds legend. A local kid who wore his United heart on his sleeve, he grew up idolising Billy Bremner and eventually took on the great man's mantle.

David Wetherall will always have a place in Leeds fans' hearts for heading the goal that gave United their first home win over Manchester United in 14 years.

Chances of silverware have been thin on the
ground since 1992 but there have been some
exceptional strikers.

Jimmy Hasselbaink was always spectacular and never lost for an opinion.

Tony Yeboah had the most powerful shot since
Peter Lorimer and his fierce 25-yard volley
against Liverpool has been voted United's best
ever goal.

Mark Viduka's four-goal demolition of Liverpool ensured his place in the Elland Road Hall of Fame.

We watched local-hero Alan Smith grow from a precocious teenager into a Premiership star. He swears he will be back one day.

In an age when players move clubs almost as often as David Beckham changes hair styles, Gary Kelly and Lucas Radebe stand out for their loyal service to the cause.

South Africa skipper Radebe overcame injury and homesickness – and almost got used to the cold at Thorp Arch – to become one of the Premiership's top central defenders and a great ambassador for Leeds and football.

Leeds were close to sending Gary Kelly home because they thought he wouldn't make it as a forward, but Howard Wilkinson had the idea to move him to right back and within a season the teenager was playing in the World Cup. His emotional testimonial saw a packed house raise £655,000 for cancer charities in memory of his sister Mandy.

Leeds teams have had some great goalkeepers over the years. Gary Sprake got his chance as a teenager and became a regular in the Revie era. Gary made some fine saves but was also prone to errors on big occasions.

Lucas Radebe twice stepped into the breach during matches and showed he was almost as good with his hands as he was with feet and head.

It can be lonely being a goalkeeper. John Lukic felt the eerie silence when United were forced to play behind closed doors (although one man got in!)

Dave Stewart was left wondering if the others were still out there in the fog or had the game been called off?

They say goalkeepers have to be slightly mad but it looks as though Nigel Martyn, one of Leeds' best ever keepers, has questions about team-mate Jon Woodgate.

It's a great life being a keeper, especially when you've just headed the winning goal!

And it's hard to stop smiling when you've just shown you've got what it takes in your first full game in front of 67,000 at Old Trafford.

When you look through the who's who of Leeds United there are some names that are not so familiar but they also serve.

Alex Sabella

Andy Watson

Phil Hughes

David McNiven

114

George McCluskey

Andy Williams

Lyndon Simmonds

Noel Whelan

Derek Lilley

Phil Masinga

Jamie Forrester

Clyde Wijnhard

Jeff Chandler

Winning trophies is what it is all about but sometimes they turn up in some strange places. Norman Hunter positioned the Players' Player of the Year trophy to guard his near post as son Michael shot at goal.

Margaret Clarke and Pat Charlton use the FA Cup as an ice bucket on the way home in 1972.

A footballer's life is not all glamour. There's hanging around at airports.

And waiting around for the FA Cup draw, though it's a mistake to celebrate too soon, especially when you've just heard you've got Colchester away.

Trying to get fit can mean getting on your bike.

Although race enthusiast David Batty preferred a
Grand Prix bike under him.

Not content with great action shots,
photographers always want those offbeat
pictures they think the public will love.
And, of course, they want to know what you are
doing after you've hung up your boots.

Chapter Four

On the spot – the moment of truth

F ew things in football concentrate the attention as much as a penalty or free-kick around the penalty box. The build up of tension and its release – in joy or disappointment – is palpable.

The changes in football technology have led to an increased number of goals from free-kicks from 25 or even 30 metres out. Players like Ian Harte have mastered the technique of getting the ball high enough to beat the wall but with that dip that keeps it under the bar. But even before manufacturers made life even harder for keepers with lighter, more manoeuvrable balls, players like Peter Lorimer and Johnny Giles found a way to punish careless fouls.

Penalties bring the game down to a gladiatorial contest, a battle of nerve and wits between the taker and the keeper, with the expectations weighing heavily on the man on the spot.

Peter Lorimer is Leeds United's penalty king and, as we can see from the casual attitude of the Arsenal defenders (and the referee), no one expected him to miss.

He was difficult for keepers to 'pick' because he could put them either side, side-foot or blasted, with equal ease and deadly accuracy.

Lorimer's free-kicks were equally effective. His '90 miles an hour' nickname was well earned which explains the apprehensive look on the faces of the Derby 'wall' as they stand just ten yards away.

Peter Lorimer scored 238 goals for United, 81 more than the next highest goalscorer, John Charles. Yet he is probably almost as well remembered for two shots that didn't count.

In the 1973 FA Cup final, the Wembley crowd and the millions watching on TV, were stunned when Sunderland keeper Jim Montgomery somehow managed to make a breathtaking double save, the second from a close range Lorimer thunderbolt.

A year later 'Lorro' struck an unstoppable free-kick past Bayern Munich keeper Sepp Maier in the European Cup final only for the referee and linesman to rule it out for a dubious offside and the team collected losers' medals.

Billy Bremner's expression sums up the feeling of the Leeds team after their European Cup defeat in Paris.

Johnny Giles was another who could be equally devastating from free-kicks or penalties.

Danny Granville's first touch of the ball as a Leeds player was in a UEFA Cup penalty shoot-out that saw United scrape through against Maritimo.

As with everything else, Frank Worthington took spot kicks with style.

In recent years, Ian Harte became a penalty and
free-kick specialist and anything within range
meant a tough time for the opposition defence.

Of course every side has its free-kick specialist
and there are times when you are in the wall,
though with the rapid turnover of players, it is
hard to find anyone in this picture who is now
at Leeds.

Chapter Five

The fans – forever Leeds

Players, managers and even directors come and go but the one sure thing about a football club is that the fans stay loyal, especially at Leeds United.

Never has this been more evident than in the last few years when 'living the dream' turned into a nightmare.

As the hope of becoming one of the leading clubs in Europe evaporated and was followed by relegation, the revolving door at Elland Road sometimes spun too fast for the eye to see.

But still the Leeds faithful remained firm, still they invested in season tickets and swore to follow their club through thick and thin.

There was a time when a lunatic fringe made Leeds supporters the most feared in the country and shamed the club.

Thankfully that passed and now Leeds United fans are admired for their loyalty and devotion to the cause.

The last few pages of our book are dedicated to you, the Leeds United supporters.

Sometimes the sun looks as though it will shine forever.

Whether it is a celebration or close-up action, every eye is focused on the pitch.

Sometimes being at a match is just a job and not always very interesting.

Sometimes that job can make you wonder if this is why you decided to join the force.

Don Revie's team were among the first to become as popular as pop stars, with all that meant in crowd control.

United fans are there, whatever the day.

They follow their side in Europe or at home,
and love the feeling of Marching On Together.

Acknowledgments

Leeds United Football Club would like to thank:

Andrew Varley of Varley Picture Agency for supplying the photographs.

Gosnay's Sports Agency of Horsforth, Leeds, for research and editorial copy.

Peter Francomb and Jonathan Davies of GreenPark Publishing for the design, artwork and printing of the book.

Photos: copyright Andrew Varley (www.vpa.uk.com).